AF447483

The Daughter of Sisyphus and Other Voices

The Daughter of Sisyphus and Other Voices

Poems by
Ashleigh Marie Pritchard

Copyright © 2012 by Ashleigh Marie Pritchard.

Cover illustration copyright © 2024 by Ashleigh Marie Pritchard.

All rights reserved. No part of this publication may be reproduced, stored in a retrieval system, or transmitted in any form or by any means—electronic, mechanical, photocopy, recording or any other—except for brief quotations in reviews, without prior permission of the publisher.

For more information, including permission to use or reproduce, please email publisher@ashleighmpritchard.com.

Printed in the United States of America.

ISBN-13: 979-8-218-55121-6

Ebook ISBN-13: 979-8-3305-4554-4

Revised 2025.

Contents

III.

Dedication

This collection is dedicated to those who supported me through the writing (and submitting) process, to Julie Sheehan, and to Adam.

Kind Words

"It is a welcome relief to read a young poet not completely wrapped up in the person worls of the "I." [...] This is a poet of notable accomplishment and immense promise."

— *Billy Collins*

"[T]he poet demonstrates a strong sense of the arc of a poem. [...] She should be commended for her empathy with others and for her ability to put that empathy into strong and well-crafted poetry."

— *Harvey Shapiro*

Foreward

I finished writing these words in 2012.

I'm writing this foreward on November 6, 2024, and these pages feel just as relevant today as they did when I wrote them over twelve years ago.

Oops. I never thought I'd go this long without writing something creative and substantial.

Writing just got harder to fit into my day. Life got busy. I struggled with my own chronic illness, and with my spouse's mental illness. I started my own business. (Making your own hours is less appealing when you know you're the only one there to get it all done.) I lost touch with writer friends.

But these poems have been collecting moss for too long. They deserve to be published, to be out in the world being read, where they were intended to be.

Especially as I try to wrap my head around how the world and this country got here, it's important to me that my words reach someone. Who knows what the future of books looks like. This might be my last chance to publish for some time to come.

There are lots of ways to fight back. Words are one of them.

These are fighting poems.

The Daughter of Sisyphus and Other Voices

I.

Imaginary Paintings
after Lisel Mueller

I
HOW THE RIVER WOULD PAINT TIME
I reach up to the coastline and beyond,
wiping away houses and families in a place
where houses and families should have never been built.

II
HOW WE WANT TO PAINT MARRIAGE
Anything painted in the style of Seurat, where tiny moments
of paint slide from harmony into discord
the farther away you are.

III
HOW THE CHILD WILL PAINT HUNGER
I'm here, eating away at you
so you can't ignore me anymore
because I need you almost as much
as you need me.

IV
HOW TO PAINT DISAPPOINTMENT
Build yourself up. Then reach high,
higher, until you find something, anything,
and then wait for a fall that isn't coming and never will.

V
IF SHE COULD HAVE DRAWN HATE
A hasty sketch on a scrap page
ripped from a notebook and taped to a wall,
trying to fill the space of some vast
canvas never painted.

VI
THE AMERICAN DREAM PAINTS ITSELF,
starts with gray, then slowly works it apart.
exposes it as the union of overpowering black
and the loneliness of white.

VII
HOW I WOULD PAINT REALIZATION
The life of an annual—
Plant seeds. The roots take hold.
Branches poke out and begin to bud,
and if you're lucky, a single bloom.

The Treachery of Text

A poem does not exist
in the ink of letters.
Instead, it lives in moments.

A poem hides, in the sinuous sound
of the s, the shelter
of the e, the texture

of the x. Sometimes, it yells
at the top of your lungs.
Sometimes it whispers.

Sometimes it finds you like death:
whether you're ready
or not.

This is not a poem.

Defending Beauty
for Carl Sagan

Walt Whitman says that science ruins
the perception of beauty. My father says that beauty
exists because of God.

On clear nights, I watch the stars
in their choreography around the horizon. I know
that because their light has come from lightyears away,
through wispy galaxies and lonely space and glowing nebulae,
that I am seeing into their past;

that when stars die, all the dust
they created over a lifetime is lost to space,
floating like dandelion seeds caught in a solar wind,
glowing, incandescent with the energy
of a new generation of stars formed from the ashes;

that the same stardust, caught
in the swirling, luminous hold of gravity,
coalesced to form you and I;

and I say there is beauty in knowledge.

I am the daughter of Sisyphus

What the legend does not tell
is that the boulder wasn't always a punishment
but a token, standing tall on its mountain,
a warrior, a man, blunt and strong and old,
a reminder to those below to always be
better than themselves. Until one day, it fell:
casualty of a man who breaks the confidence
of the gods. The earth shifts under a man with shifting
morals. And so Sisyphus created
his own punishment, trying to undo
what can never be undone.

Thus he stands—here will Sisyphus spend
the rest of his days, and maybe the days after, trying to restore
what his own *hybris* destroyed, captivated
by the belief that all can be put right,
that one day, he'll push hard enough
and right enough and just enough
to return the mountain to balance,
and each fallen piece will come back to him.

He hopes I will come back, too.
Like the gods, I have no compassion
for the man who lives a life of penance
that has been rightfully earned.

The Act of Reading

She whispers
and invites me into the space
between her letters,
waiting to be unfolded
from the petals of words
and I, like my 7-year-old self
in the corner of the play-
ground, happily oblige,
and pull each page away
as I search for the yellow
pollen center, whispering
with each one, "She loves me,
she loves me not,
she loves me..."

Sonata for Summer Afternoons
A Storm in Three Movements

I. Exposition
There are quiet notes
before a storm in August,
when the distant thunder
begins its beat. Static
and perspiration
hang in the air, and
then the droplets fall,
slow at first—*piano*—
a theme of metal in the key
of cars, street lights and tin
roofs.
II. Development
The trickle of sound
builds into one harmonious
chorus, an orchestra
of trees like reeds, thunder,
and the wooden timbre
of chimes, then—*allegro*—
the raindrops fall
faster, faster, the downpour
peaks, notes drowning
out notes, a concert
and Earth, the instrument,
all song, and—*crescendo*—
at once the notes
surround and inundate
and surge in chords and the wind
plays deep and throaty
through branches and leaves;
a great cacophony of storm,
until, a flash—*fortissimo*—
the great boom of percussion
shakes the stage below with
vibrato, and again,
again; the thick tumult
of metal and wood and rain
blended with the deep
rolling resonance of lightning's drum.

III. Recapitulation
Later—*diminuendo*—
the thunder recedes into the distance
its percussive refrain hushed
to a murmur, the last note
of an echo almost
lost, while—*adagio*—
the patter of the rain becomes
again its dulcet rhythm, its
metallic hymn, mixed
with the dripping eaves
and the guttural drop of water
into water.

Rusted

At twenty-seven, you inherited a bike
already choked with rust.

You push each pedal
with all your strength
and listen to the gears
chirp and whine.
Push, push, they labor
back and forth along
this dead-end street. They struggle
to meet your demands,
to meet the demands of a road
strewn with gravel and warped
by hills, in the same way
you struggle, though you'll never notice.

Fire Safety for the Fourth of July

We unfurl a blanket
under a maple's ponderous mid-summer
leaves. Fireworks fill the sky, light
and sound. Together we watch the embers
streak down and settle. And we let
the rhythm rock us to sleep.

Beyond our closed eyes
the falling embers set fire to the grass,
and the flame laps at the sides
of our cottony raft. It carries us away,

and we let it. We dream
in the swell of the waves and the crackle
of the burning country-
side and we don't notice
when the edges of our lifeboat
catch flame. The fire eats away and we stay
asleep, though it threatens to burn us, too.

If we're lucky, the scars will be small,
superficial, and permanent.

Ordinance on Arrival
after Naomi Lazard

"Give me your tired, your poor,
your huddled masses yearning to breathe free..."
                    —Inscription on the Statue of Liberty

Welcome to the United States. As a precaution,
please fill out the following form as accurately
as possible. If you need an interpreter, please skip
directly to the bottom of this form.

Your name, using only the approved
American English alphabet ________________________________
If your name includes non-approved
characters, or is difficult
to pronounce, please write "No" in the blank: ________

Your race: White   or   No

Your economic situation: I have a job   or   I am a job seeker
Please be aware that jobs are only
available to natural-born citizens of the U.S.
and any immigrants found taking jobs
away from true Americans will be removed
from their homes, prosecuted, and sent
to their country of birth or the nearest
Spanish-speaking country.

Taxpayer assistance: If you intend to take advantage
of any public schools, hospital care including the maternity
ward, welfare, food stamps, housing assistance,
driving a car, imbibing clean water,
flushing a toilet, turning on a light-bulb
or other electrical appliance, or applying
for citizenship, please note these services are exclusive.
Food, water, housing and medical care
are privileges restricted for those
who are American enough to pay for them
on their own. If you have not earned
the privilege, please write "No" in the blank: ________

Language: The United States' official language is American
English and any other languages are
unacceptable. If you speak any other language,

or if you are unable to speak American
English fluently and without any hint
of dialect or accent, please write "No" in the blank: ________

Religion: The United States' official religion is Christianity,
but only the kind that has morals. If you are required
to fill out this form, you must be an illegal
immigrant and therefore, clearly, have no
morals. Please write "No" in the blank: ________

Thank you for your time. If you answered
"No" to any of the questions above,
your presence in this country has been denied.
Any protestation will be seen as an act of war
against the United States, you will be labeled
a terrorist, and any opportunity you hoped
to have for yourself or your family
will be confirmed to have never existed.

We apologize for the inconvenience. Your
family has been contacted and we would be
more than happy to offer you a ride
back to wherever you came from, and we
wish you the best in your future,
as long as it's not here.

II.

Salem: 1990, The First Intifada, at 7

They came again last night,
in tanks that chewed the leftover crumbs
of our city in their wheel-teeth
while I was pretending to sleep.
I could hear them through the walls
roaring and spewing and smoking and smashing
three more houses, like they were made of Legos.

Outside my window in the morning,
there's white dust that hides the street
like snow—I've never
seen real snow, but the white dust,
it looks just like it—

Mama tells me, Don't play
with the stones and don't touch those steel
rods sticking out of the dirt,
but there's no where else
to go. Ayham and me, we
play army doctor where the houses
once stood, fighting off the Jews
and looking for people
buried alive.

I find a teddy bear, covered
in the dust-snow and he's got an eye
hanging off. We can't save him,
so we name him Mohammed,
wrap him in white and green,
and rejoice.

Hernando: 1993, Business Trip, at 8

There used to be pigs here.
Fields of pigs: *Mamá* pigs and *papá* pigs
and baby pigs all covered
in little white hair.
Pig families, all together.

Once, *Papá* told me stories
about when he was a little boy
on the farm with *Abuelo*.
Everybody worked on the farm.
They grew *maíz* and tomatoes and pigs.

Now, *Papá* says there are cheaper pigs,
and that's why the pigs went away
The pigs went away, so the people went away.
There's no more pigs and that's why
there's no more people. *Papá* left, too, this morning.
So it's just me and *Mamá* and José Carlos and Isabella.

Papá went where they all went: *el norte.*
Papá says he will come home.
Mamá says he will come home,
when he's raised enough money.

Hernando: *1994, The Desert, at 9*

Mamá says there's a letter from *Papá*.
It's twenty kilometers
to the post office, so she says
it will take all day. I ask her
if she will see *Papá* there, but she says no.
She says he's even more far away than that.

José Carlos and me, we sit on the steps
and see who can throw rocks the best
into the empty pig fields.
It's quiet so we can hear *Mamá* coming
before she gets to our street and we run out
to meet her. What did he send, *Mamá*?
What did he send? She has an envelope in her hand
but it's wet and crinkled, like her face.
She says she got a letter, and that *Papá*
isn't coming home. She says
the desert liked *Papá* so much
he decided to stay.

Where's *Papá*? I ask.
Where's *Papá*? but she doesn't answer,
just hugs me hard and hides the letter
from the man named Coroner.

Terence: 1995, Deposit, at 9

and best part of going to the grocery store
with Daddy is riding the carts,
wait till it's really full then you
push real hard and jump on
with your arms up like   flying.

Daddy tells me to stop but I tell him about the flying
and he says, There's some things you aint ever gonna get to do
and flying's one of them.

I tell him the teacher at school says I aint ever
gonna go to college, neither, cause theres no
poor people in college, and he says
course you going. He points
to the giant pickles under the Fruit Loops
and you and me, we gonna save and save and fill
that whole jar up with money, he says.

I wanna start   now I say.
So we go home and put the pickles in a bag
and Daddy writes "College Fund"
in big letters and puts it on the bookshelf

so it stares back down at me

empty

like a cut

Salem: 1995, Exit Strategies, at 12

Mama says I'm leaving this place,
but she doesn't say when.

I run down the street,
short-cut through an empty house
to find Ayham. The dust is gone
from the street and the houses
since the tanks left the village
No more tanks for almost a month.
No more snow.

I find Ayham on the steps cleaning
a gun. It is a gift! he calls to me.
A birthday gift from my brother.
—Behind him is Mohammed the teddy bear,
still wrapped in his green scarf—

We hear bullets in the backyard firing so fast they hum.
I grab Mohammad and we find a place to hide under a table,
but it's too late.
Ayham's shirt is red.
His hands are red and shaking
and his eyes are open, staring at me.

I put the green scarf over Ayham's eyes and tell him
everything's going to be okay.

Salem: 1996, Child of Gaza, at 13

If I could, I would tell him,
Ayham, I've seen the snow,
the real snow! It's cold and gleaming
and cleansing and you'll love it
when you get here.

I would tell him how
on my first day in an American school
the teacher made me stand up
in front of all the other kids
and tell what it was like living in Israel.
—I kept saying that I didn't live in Israel
that I lived in Palestine—
She laughed at me and she told me that Palestine isn't a real country,
that Palestine is home for criminals and insurgents and terrorists
that Israel is the country, and here in America, she said,
we support Israel and that means me.
She said that I was lucky to get out alive
and I had better sit back down.

I didn't want to fight anymore,
so I took my seat and wondered why
I deserved to be lucky and you didn't.

Rose: 1998, Hormones, at 11

There are three different kinds of tears.
The simplest tears are for comfort and ease
of vision. Some clear out irritants in our eyes;
others clean out irritants
in our thoughts. These so-called emotional
tears release a chemical compound
used by the body to alleviate pain
in times of stress.

The saline in tears helps
conduct electricity, not enough
to kill you, or even enough
for you to really feel anything at all.
Tears are alkaline—or, for the less
scientific, basic, that is, having a high
pH—and consequently
rather the opposite of acidic,
but against my cheek, feel corrosive
nonetheless.

          Crying is a defense
mechanism, according to some
anthropologists or biologists or sociologists.
Tears are sometimes involuntary and can
secrete hormones in order
to let others know I'm vulnerable.
It's often difficult to overcome this
fact of my biology. Intense crying leaves
tear ducts red and inflamed,
and the runny nose can persist
several minutes later. Though crying
is often associated with catharsis
and feelings of rejuvenation, it is well
substantiated that those who feel shame
for crying often feel worse afterward.

Terence: *1998, Revolving, at 12*

so's the prep school across in Harlem
has five spots for scholarship students
and Dad says they's the best
chance to get me to college.

Says kids who go there,
they don't need money
to go. Says being the best in a worst
school won't cut it. Like there's two
kinds of people: the ones who's
got somewhere waiting for them,
someplace they're meant to end up,
and then there's the ones who's stuck.
The ones dug into the ground
with no way out who might be
the smart one in a family or a house
or the whole street, the ones
who's said about them that they should've
had someplace to go, too,
and maybe they did something
to lose it or maybe they didn't want it
and they better off here anyway.

We filled out the papers and sent them
for the lottery. They told us we're one of 1,347.
I put the pen in the pickle jar
on top of the pennies, hoping maybe
there's something other than money
that'll get me outta this place,
cause there aint no money here.

Says this's the only chance cause
they don't take no one who's in high school already,
or who went to the high school
and was one of the smart ones
and got out.

Hernando: **2000, Crossing, at 13**

We need money, *Mamá* says.
We always need money. There are no jobs
at home, so I went where they all went: *el norte.*
In the village, I heard the men and the women
whisper about America, the wonderful America!
It led me there, in the Arizona desert
three weeks away from home, lost.

We walked at night, hoping the dark
would hide us from police eyes.
But the dark is dishonest
and led us in the wrong direction.

It gets cold here at night, so cold
I could see myself breathing. I didn't think
to pack a blanket, but even if I had
there wouldn't have been room.
The water only lasted three days, and the last loaf
of bread was stale at four. It doesn't rain here.

This jail cell is comforting tonight, the warm, the food.
And tomorrow, after the bus takes me home,
I'll know better. I'll know better
so that next time, I'll make it.

*Elaina: **2000, The Scent of Honeysuckle, at** 11*

For recess, we sit under
the honeysuckle
and watch boys.

I pick off the sweet flowers
and suck their juice.
The other girls
pick out the boys
they are going to marry.
Chrissy swears her undying love
for Alex Moore and asks
What about Elaina?
I throw a pile of sucked-dry
flowers and answer,
Boys are lame.

Chrissy laughs.
Her eyes are the color
of honeysuckle and
patches of sunshine.
I want to tell her
they're pretty. I want to
tell her I'd drink them right up,
but they're busy,
staring at Alex Moore.

Salem: 2001, Fall Back, at 18

The world is dust.
I'm covered in it, and I breathe it,
dust made of concrete and metal, fire and death.
I can feel the screams all around,
but I cannot hear them.
The dust isolates.

It is almost a blessing
that I cannot see what's been lost.
I can sense the void, and that is enough. These tears do little
to wash away the dust. They mix
more like cement
than water.

Rose: 2003, Chemical, at 16

Happiness is caused by a chemical
in the brain called serotonin,
the doctor tells me. She says
depression means I don't have enough
serotonin. She says my body knows
eating foods high in sugar
increases the chemical's presence in my nervous
system. It's normal, she says, for people like me
to crave sugar, that people with depression
often self-medicate.

I ask if it's normal
to mix a bowl of cookie dough,
refrigerate it, and save it
for later consumption, raw. Cookie
dough was meant to be baked, but when chilled,
the dough becomes creamy and frothy and so
sweet. She says it's just my body
trying to feel happy again.

Dough is mostly sugar,
the substance she says I crave,
but when mixed properly,
one finds, folded inside in hidden
dimensions are the subtle hints
of molasses, vanilla, and butter.
I've had years to perfect the recipe.
On special occasions,
I drop neat spoonfuls on a cookie sheet
and slide them in the oven,
just to see what happens.

Hernando: *2003, Crossing Over, at 17*

The *coyote* howls,
warns us to guard our heads
against the helicopter lights.
Two years to save,
to hire this wolf of the border
to get me across, to get me
to *el norte*, and still the same:

The same wide, night skies,
framed by hard horizons
and cactus thorns. Wide
empty skies. Empty like pig fields.
Always cloudless,
like the dry ground whispers up,
tells the rain to stay away,
that there are better places than this bald,
this wasteland, to take such a favor.
The rain. The smell of wet earth,
the restoring rain, the touch of cool water.
My mouth misses water.

Coyote moves like a wolf,
calls us in grunts and growls to follow,
quick, agile, eyes open to the darkness.
His hair is gray and stiff,
and he is dangerous to cross.

Terence: *2003, Overdrawn, at 18*

with the two open envelopes
side by side
on the table and a beer in his hand.
I force a bag of the day's work
clothes next to him and he says
I got in but he should've bought
a bigger jar. It's half-full
and there's a dry ball-point pen
buried somewhere underneath.
I ask him what's in the other letter
and he doesn't answer, just
swigs some more beer

and breathes like he knows

he's only got so many left.

Elaina: **2004, The Sound of Rejection, at 15**

If I could, I would go back
and never say it.
I would never tell her
how much I loved her,
her laugh, the light
in her honeysuckle eyes.

Her parents called and told me
to stay away.
My father said with shaking hands
that I didn't pray enough.
My mother was quiet while
she packed my suitcase; and then:
I don't care where, but not here,
not in this house.
The bed creaked under the weight of it.

The other kids know now. They all know.
They call me names to my face,
fag and dyke and sinner.
The senior boys slip notes in my locker
and meet me outside the girls bathroom
in the science wing to remind me
they know just what I need
to strip the gay right out of me.

Rose: *2004, SSRI, at 18*

These pills are white
and round
and small;
they are so small
for such a chore.
These pills are meant
to repair the imbalance
of chemicals in my brain;
of emotions in my brain.
Escitalopram oxalate 20 mg
once a day
and I'm supposed
to be happy
again, supposed to feel
relief from pain,
insomnia, and lethargy,
supposed to clear
my mind of dangerous
thoughts. The medication
mechanically increases the creation
of serotonin to flood
the synapses of my brain,
the voids between neurons
where contentment should be.

Salem: 2005, The Second Intifada, at 22

The voices came again last night:
Terrorist! Terrorist!
They yell at me in my sleep.

I see them, getting on the subway,
or walking the streets. They stare at me.
I hear voices through their eyes.
They think they're angry at me,
but all I see is the yelling.

All I hear is their fear. I'm afraid that one day,
it will crumble them, right in front of me,
that just the sound of me will reduce them to rubble,
and then I really will be a terrorist.

I rehearse the speech in my head, explaining
I'm not one of them, that I'm American, too.
—I'm studying to be a doctor.
I want to save people, not kill them—

I wish I could have saved Ayham, too.
Some nights, he's there, in the crowd,
not yelling but watching. His eyes
are full of the same weight, the same rubble.
Terrorist! they yell. Ayham watches. His tears are silent.
Maybe they're all right.

*Elaina: **2008, The Touch of Water, at 19***

Kate twists her hand into mine
as we stroll the boardwalk.
Miles from the house I dread,
I breathe salt air and revel
in the sting of it, the wonderful
sting of her desire to care for me.
She's the land. I was drowning,
and she saved me. She's the wide,
striking sand between my bare toes
as we drift onto the beach.

No, not really. That sounds ridiculous.
It's more that she stood by
and encouraged me (in a way I could not
on my own) to save myself.

She breaks into a sprint
and begs me to follow like she
doesn't know the answer.
We run through the sand, feeling
the richness of it on our feet,
bits of softened glass and rock,
the sterile dust of dead creatures,
shell and bone. Foamy waves
slide up the beach and kiss us.
Sand, water, sand, water.   The shore
dirties us and then rinses us clean.

*Elaina: **2008, The Taste of Apples, at 20***

Side by side, we lean over the double
porcelain sink in our kitchen
and peel the apples we chose
from the orchard down Esworthy
for a dollar a pound.
She turns the news on in the background.
I tell her it doesn't matter,
but she insists.

We blend butter and flour in clumsy
harmony—She wants apple pie,
though neither of us know how to make it.
We are too young to have known the years
when mothers had taught their daughters
to cook. We figured once we had the red
fruit, fleshy and fertile, that it should come to us.—
We put the two pies in the oven,
and she watches while she waits,
twisting her ring in pirouettes around her finger.
Reports come in, San Fransisco, Napa, Los Angeles.

I'm not hungry anymore.
She steps out into the cold night and tries
to breathe deep. I swallow a tepid
glass of water, try to rinse
the barren taste from my mouth.
We leave them on the kitchen counter,
the two misshapen pies,
and forget about them.

Hernando: 2008, Routine, at 21

American constitutes a piece of paper,
an accent, and a skin color.
I have none. I will never earn
American. In the village, we imagined
the attitude was all we'd need
to blend in. But nothing
evicted the glares, nothing
drove out the sound
of beaner, chicano, wetback,
as police rounded us up.
They tell me I must stay
in *México*, that I am a criminal,
and if I try to return home, jail
waits for me. *Mamá* calls,
tells me my old room will be ready,
but I tell her not to bother
because I'm not staying long.

Terence: *2009, Collection, at 24*

when cleaning out Dad's old stuff,
and there it was: *We are pleased
to inform you*   There's a deposit
of dust and there's places where "fund"
is starting to rub off. I can't hardly
lift the trash, take it out to the curb
and leave it.

Rose: *2010, Signs, at 23*

If you know someone with depression,
watch closely for the following
behavioral warnings:
Withdrawal from family or friends, whether
gradual or sudden;
A lack of interest in previously-enjoyed
activities, such as social outings to Harvard's,
or a lack of energy or involvement;
The loss of self-esteem, hope, caution, or personal
care routines, for example, the application of
under-eye concealer and brown eyeliner;
A sudden sense of peace, resolve, or finality;
Changes in appetite, desire, or hunger,
as in instances of skipping meals; and
A preoccupation with death, dying, or end-of-life
arrangements, such as giving away special possessions,
particularly the ruby necklace inherited
from a grandmother who died of suicide.

The signs of suicidal thoughts
are rather pervasive but are often
overlooked for a number of reasons.
Some sufferers shield their distress
by overcompensating for their naturally depressive
state. Some act out. Some mask their feelings
with excessive energy. Alternatively,
those who do little to hide suicidal
tendencies are often ignored by family
members and friends who do not recognize
the signs, or who incorrectly believe
that although sufferers may desire attention
the likelihood of an actual attempt
is absurd. With the social
stigma attached to depression and related
issues, it is no wonder so few seek treatment
for this life-threatening illness.

III.

Binary

Two stars orbit
in a state called equilibrium,
but it is only temporary.
The empty space
between them shrinks.
Gravity has taken hold,
and there is no escape.

Two stars orbit
closer and closer,
and lose their shape.
Each pulls on the other,
siphons matter and energy
in the attempt to grow.
They blur the lines between one
and the other, consuming, the way
I am afraid of being consumed by you.

A letter to Sisyphus

You have been at this for months.

Don't you tire
of walking the same walk,
talking the same talk?
Surely by now you know
every crevice of your stone,
every jut of your mountain,
every contusion on your feet.
What else have you left to learn?

Appeal to the Consumer

We've been together so long,
you and I. We've spent the last years
investing in our future,
building interest in each other.

You've always kept me in your life,
always supported me, funded me,
helped me grow.
We never go anywhere without each other.
You took me into account through college,
our first car, our first house,
and I stuck with you, through the medical bills,
the taxes, the unemployment, the defaults.

Because of you, I've prospered,
and I want you to know
that you deserve all the credit.
When we met, I was insignificant,
pocket change. And now,
I'm growing every day,
exponentially. All I needed
was your validation.

So if you're going to withdraw from me,
at least let's keep it on good terms.

Toll Road

Traffic clogs the one-lane road,
cars crawling as one,
like a great tapeworm

growing and writhing through
the bowels of the city.
There are faces here,

among the monotony of broken
buildings, people who carry their lives
in a shopping bag, like the boy

who taps my passenger window,
a bill crumpled in one hand,
payment for a ride out.

Wildfire

It hasn't rained in 63 days.
The trees are thirsty
and the wind is blowing low and strong,
perfect for sparking and spreading
the flames and the smoke,
billowing into the air,
winding into windows
and doors so you can't breathe
and the deer and the foxes hide
under porches and think they're safe
as the orange flames grip
nearby trees and whatever
water was hiding inside
becomes steam and is lost.
My skin is dry, too.
Perfect for burning.

To the poet

I write poems
but I am not a poet.
Because you are a poet,

& if I'm a poet
& you're a poet,
then we're both poets,

& that puts our poetry
in the same arena & our poems
in the same category, & I don't think my poems
are quite up to the challenge. So let's call it a draw
                 & have a rematch between my poems
& your poetry
for some other day & some other year down the line
                 & we'll finally know who the real poet
is & who simply writes poems
because there's a difference between the person who writes a poem

or two & the person whose life is the poem.
So let's keep writing & I'll write my poems
& you'll write your poetry

& maybe one day I'll be a poet
like you're a poet
& I'll write poems
by living.

The Lepidopterist

The butterfly is a cycle
of entrapment and escape,
often self-inflicted,
sometimes inflicted by a curious six-year-old
with a Mason jar and no shoes,
but always mandatory.

It struggles against the glass
and the metal lid with the three air holes
made by a father with a nail and hammer.
Perhaps one day, if it hasn't died, she'll release it.

OCD

Wrap the leftover food in airtight
containers. Listen for the last breaths
of air from the plastic bags. Slide a finger
around ceramic lips to seal the Saran wrap.
Scrape plates clean; throw out portions
too small to be considered leftovers.
Wipe sticky sauces and dressing
from bowls with half a paper towel

        Empty the trash.
        Walk it out into the idle February
        air and toss it into the dumpster.

Run the water until steaming
and hot enough to kill
bacteria. Wash both hands, working
soap into the crevices and under fingernails
and into that raw cut. Next, wash the plates,
first front, then back, then the front again.
Check for persistent memories of food.
Scrub cups, wiping the sponge along the rim,
eliminating the last traces of sustenance.

Dry each dish thoroughly, reaching
the towel into each tender corner
to soak up the last drops of water. Put each away,
out of sight behind cabinet doors, spotless
and unremarkable. Leave no evidence.

Trying to Quit

I was beginning to get by without you.

And then, there you are. Watching me
from behind the window in the 7-Eleven.

I watch you, relaxed, poised,
at the check-out counter
and forget where I am.
You lean over, whisper sweet nothings
to the check-out girl.
She walks past. You feel her hair.
Her hand glides near you.

           — Did you just see me? Shit.
I reach for my phone,
check a message that isn't really there
so I don't look like an idiot
standing out in the rain
staring into the window of the 7-Eleven.

My hands miss you.
My hair still smells of you.
And I don't care that I'm better off.

A bell hangs on the door.
It rings as I enter, come to reclaim you.

A *plea for Sisyphus*

Sisyphus, you are doing things wrong.
Each muscle is meant for a different
task and in this way all muscles
are stretched and strengthened.
But you persist. You insist
that your arms are all you need
to carry the weight of this trouble
but they can't,
and they aren't meant to.

Boating after Irene

Ripples of water part at the bow, froth
and move on. Leaves hang like defeat
from dead branches, some saplings,
some a hundred years old.

The banks of this river are brick walls
and windows boarded up. Plywood
is useless against the tide, lapping
three feet above submerged zinnias.

The Pursuit

The snow spotted
with shadows and specks
of moonlight almost hid the doe's
body, her silver eyes.

I reached
for a gun that wasn't there.
No bow, no arrows,

so I stopped, savored
her presence and wondered—
if I called to her,

would she lay down at my feet;
would she give herself to me?

As she ran
her hooves left pale holes
in the ground.

Beach at Road D

Sand has worked its way
between my copper-painted
toes. Salt-air clings
heavy to my hair.
The mist grows thick,
hides the horizon
and the dunes.
Waves break from somewhere
unseen. Here in this bubble
it's hard to imagine
the world beyond—
and yet, I see the mist yield,
overpowered
by the headlights of some car.

The Scarecrow

I am held together with loose threads
and knotted stitches.
                               She kept
an assortment of metal blades
in her sewing kit—one she used
to clean up the seams she birthed—
twisted and tangled—though she labored
hours at the machine
                                 —and I her cross,
wove her into submission—became
a needle task, like a circadian rhythm—
day in, day out—in, out—around—skirting
edges—frayed and weathered from too much
wear and not enough
                                      care.
Scissors trim dead threads, loose like hair—
the needle stabs in metered beats—draws no blood,
                    leaves stitches—in my side,
                        draws a cry—
                                I hide,
hemmed in—fragmented, patched—seams
                        unfitting—
                I want to untie—to receive
the ripper—to tear myself
                        apart.

Virtual Subtext

I got the gist
of the email you sent last week.
In between hellos and thank yous and all the bests
I hear that twinge in the corner of your mouth,
that 'I'm disappointed in you' way
your eyes avoid making contact with mine.

I understand the implication
of that text message, too,
the one where you told me you were busy
but you really meant that you were too busy
for me.

I know what you meant in that Facebook status,
the one where you talked about people
in the way that we all talk about people
who we wish we didn't have to deal with.

I get them all now.
All your connotations and your hints
and your insinuations in the way you forgot
to call, or the way you forgot
to invite me, or the time I invited you and you forgot
to let me know you weren't coming.
I can read that same old subtext in your sorrys
as you touch your heart with your hand
like you're reminding me you mean it,
but all I hear is I'm sorry
I haven't gotten rid of you yet.
If you pay attention, you'll hear it, too.

From Sisyphus to his family

You left me to fight
with this boulder and this mountain
while you watch, cozy from below,
and worry about other things
and claim other burdens
though you carry nothing that I can see.

Forgiveness is a right that you continue
to deny me, but I'm going to keep pushing
until things go back to the way they always were.

Elegy for a Lost Belief

Heaven is where the living go
to find lost loved ones.

We imagine they're all together
and laughing, playing a game of Scrabble
or maybe reading the next Hunger Games
on their Kindles.
                        We imagine
they'll wait for us to get there in our own
good time, hug us, offer us a cup of tea
and some cookies, that they'll declare,
Pull up a chair! and there you'll join them
waiting inside your head until you die.

Isolation

I didn't mean it, he says.
I'm sorry.

The lie hides in his beady eyes,
in the stitches of his mouth.

I promise, he says.

I run my hand down
his velour body,
along the seam that imitates
where his spine would have been.
And he's soft and I smile,
bring him closer for a hug.

You're all I have, I whisper.

There it is again.
In his eyes.
The lie.

The threads sever easily
with a steak knife.
No more eyes,
no more lies.

He should have known
not to. He should have known
that I made him what he is,
that I made them all, even you.

Things I did while you were away for two weeks

I pulled the good-company
china out of the attic, selected a gold-leaf
wine glass, washed it, and used it for a cup
of peach-flavored V8.

Since I had no use for it, I skipped my birth control.
Don't worry, I'll start back up when you get home.

I left the bathroom door open while I showered
so I wouldn't have to turn on the fluorescent light.

I started a Twitter account and used it
to tweet about how much you hate Twitter.

I opened the window and let the fresh air
keep me cool. I'm sorry about all the pollen.

I drank wine.

Because I didn't want to wait four more months,
I pulled out my wedding ring, tried it on,
and decided I didn't have to take it off just then.

One night, I slept with the stuffed dog
I named "Kitty" when I was two,
but it made Steve the Dinosaur jealous.

I bought furniture for your office
even though you always do your work
on the living room floor.

I almost started believing in Jesus,
until I realized it was a trick
of light through the curtains.

The cat threw up around 9,
but I didn't clean it up until 11
so I could eat a bowl of Golden Grahams
and read the Sunday comics first.

I drank vodka.

I went to the grocery store,
forgot to take my wedding band off, and liked it.

I promised at least three people
we'd get together and do something
but I never went so that I didn't have
to come home alone.

Final notice to Sisyphus

Every time you tread the same path,
you only add weight to your trouble.
You are gathering dirt, Sisyphus.
It hardens along the skin, clings
to the rock and grips every crack
that you cannot see. If you're not careful,
you'll lose the mountain
to the stone.

The Children

Like yin and yang,
dark and light—

each letter on the page
cast from ink and paper,

each word nourished,
each line nurtured,

a child born in the act
of writing.

In the way that parents
pass knowledge to their children,

so the poet passes his heart
into his words.

The miracle of the poem
is not the creation of the language

but the perseverance
of thought

that keeps the poet alive
long after his death.

The Consumer's Reply

Please. Stop calling me.

I've tried ignoring you.
I gave you all my money,
my house, my car, my future.

I even tried changing my name
and moving to Tibet
to become a monk.

But you follow me everywhere,
even to the grocery store,
where the clerk gives me a sympathetic
look and sends me out empty-handed.
You got me kicked out of my apartment
that time I got pneumonia
and couldn't go to work.
Then you got me fired from work.

If I had known what you wanted
with me, I never would have given you
my number and told you to call
anytime you felt like it.

Gray Matter

It's not that
I don't have a poem in me.

It's hiding.
Buried under
remembering to buy milk
for the fourth day in a row
because I've run out of alternative breakfasts,
worrying over the power struggles
between my demure orange tabby
and the male, rescued from the wild,
who, though intimately familiar with the vet,
still insists on assertions,
                              and
imaging the birthday dinner
of lemon chicken and lopsided chocolate cake
I'm missing as I attempt to write this.

Thoughts keep my words trapped,
circling neuron after neuron
in repeating circuits,
unable to escape and find form
on paper.

Moving Boxes

I shake an old crocheted throw,
free it from the dust of five years of storage,
and put it in a cardboard box labeled blankets
where it will stay for another five years
collecting dust in a new house.

I walk the empty rooms,
stepping just right to hear the familiar
creaks in the staircase; I run my hands
over the walls Mom paid me twenty dollars
to paint when I was twelve. Now they're covered
in fingerprints and thumbtack holes.
The kitchen smells of turkey and green bean casserole.

Everything looks bigger when empty.
Growing up, the walls of my room seemed
to hold me in, contain me, but now
they're slipping away. I feel the doorknob
in my hands, feel the lock Dad
gave me when I started high school.
And now I'm paying for my own door
and my own lock, and I still call this room
my room and this lock my lock.

I leave behind the lock
and the walls and the floorboards,
and shut the door—

The State of Things

A tree grows
in the same manner as a family
and splits.

Some branches grow straight and tall,
leave long shadows at sunset
and some, like a father, reach too high
and fall first.

Then there are branches like a daughter,
ones that sprout
small and lithe, who aim
for the farthest point they can find,
but can never be rid of the trunk.

And when the height of a tree falls,
so does the rest of it,
and the sound will be heard
from miles away, and it will take
years for the last of the roots
to die so that we can
plant new seeds and try again.

Acknowledgements

One poem in this collection was previously published in *The Southampton Review* in 2012.

Other poems were submitted to several literary magazines for consideration in the years following my completion of this book. I received one response, a form rejection letter from the *Indiana Review* on a strip of paper—clearly done to save resources given the quantity of rejections they must send out during any given publication cycle.

About the Author

Ashleigh Marie Pritchard received her Masters of Fine Arts in Creative Writing and Literature from Stony Brook University in 2012, and a bachelor of art in Studio Art from McDaniel College in 2010.

She hated structure so much she left office life and started her own business, CharmCat Creative, creating pretty paper things for pretty funny people™, like silly greeting cards, stationery, and small gift items featuring her original watercolor art and writing.

She's a Maryland native who now lives in Martinsville, Virginia, with her paleontologist husband and two cats.

www.ingramcontent.com/pod-product-compliance
Lightning Source LLC
Chambersburg PA
CBHW021335160726
47994CB00007B/2705